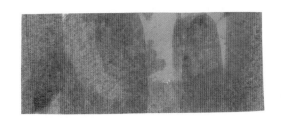

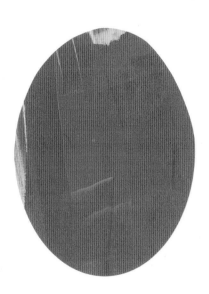

For Sallie Berry

Library of Congress Cataloging-in-Publication Data available.

ISBN 978-1-7972-0508-3

Manufactured in China.

Design by Jay Marvel.
Typeset in Brown.
The illustrations in this book were cut and collaged
from hand-painted paper and then assembled digitally.

10 9 8 7 6 5 4

Chronicle Books LLC
680 Second Street
San Francisco, California 94107

Chronicle Books—we see things differently.
Become part of our community at www.chroniclekids.com.

circle under berry

carter higgins

chronicle books · san francisco

circle under berry

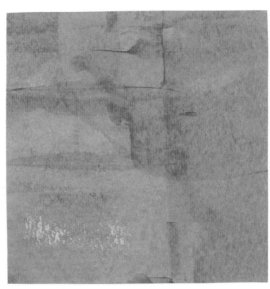

berry over square

circle over berry
under orange
over square

yellow under diamond

diamond over green

yellow over diamond
under guppy
over green

lion under scarlet

scarlet over frog

lion over scarlet
under oval
over frog

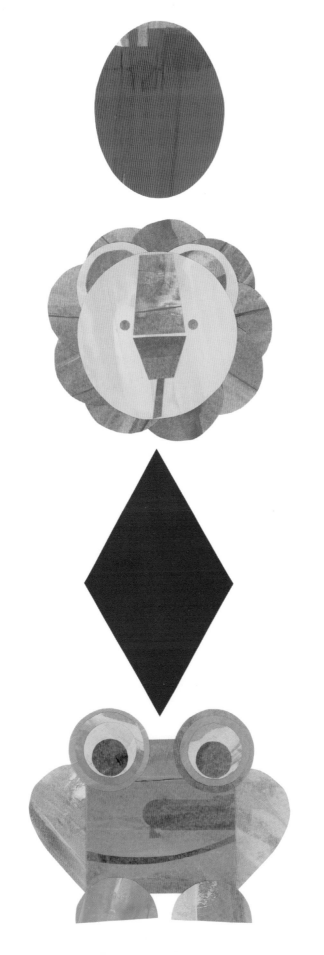

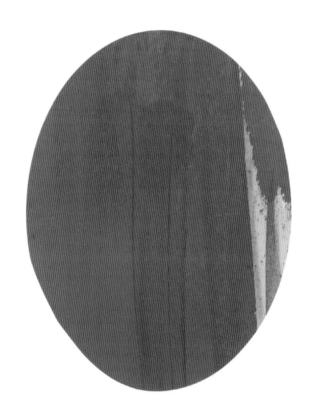

is this orange?
is it oval?

is this frog or
square or green?

and is berry over circle

or is circle under berry?

octagon this

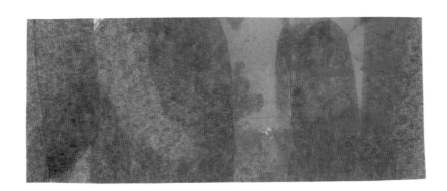

rectangle that

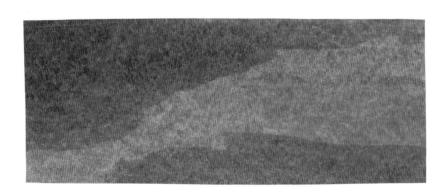

emerald left

goldenrod right

right-side-up octopus

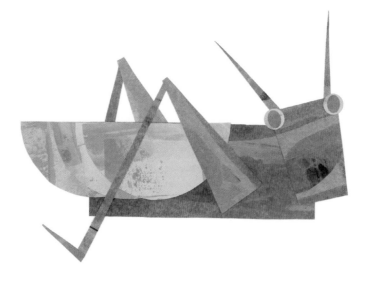

grasshopper here

upside-down octopus

there!

grasshopper

what could this octagon also become?

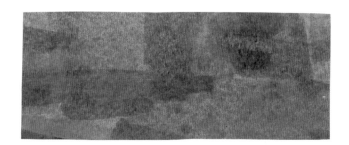

what could that rectangle be?

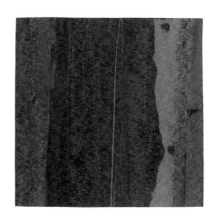

**a stack of shapes
can make you think
and wonder what you see**

circle next to berry

square by bear by sweet

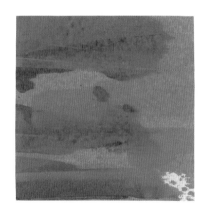

blue up high
pig down low
yellow in between

berry next to square

red by square by circle

house above
heart below
chicken in the center

circle

berry

berry

square

rose by brown by purple

**left side square
right side pink
diamond in the middle**

this one is a triangle

that one is a trapezoid

down below is indigo

magenta up above

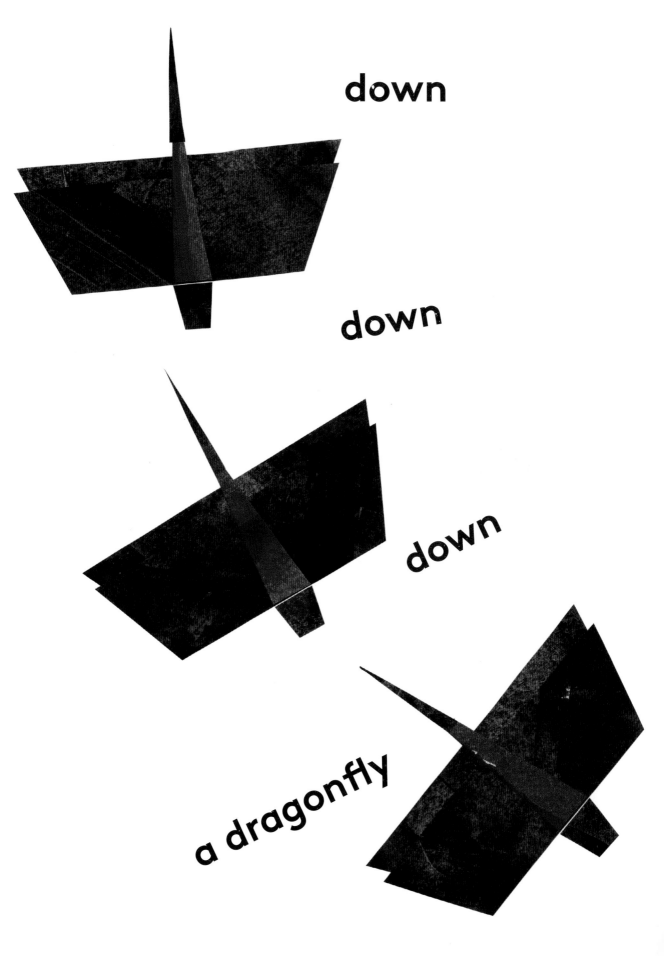

down

down

down

a dragonfly

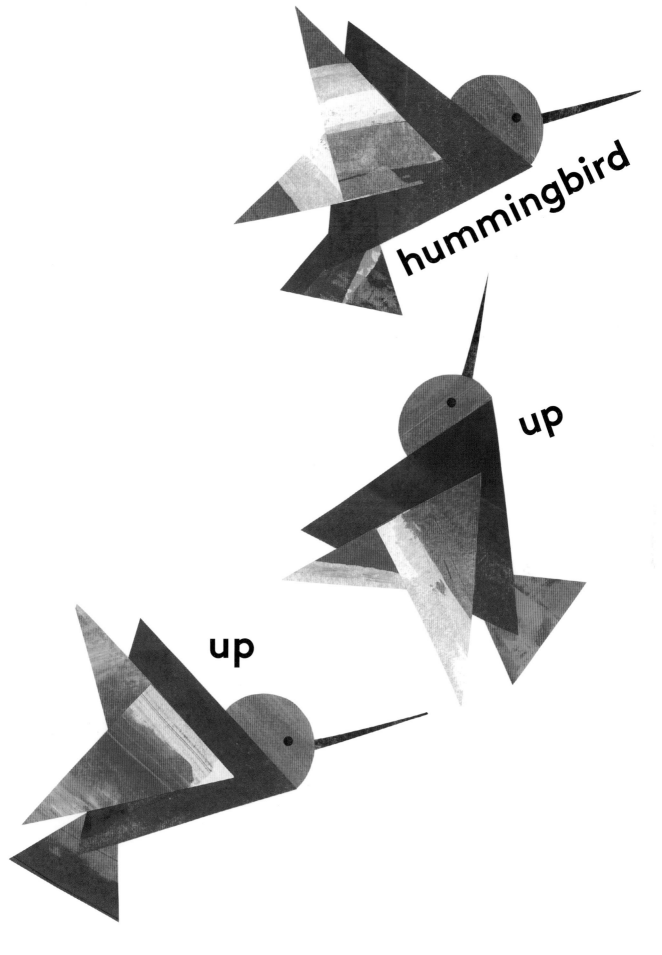

hummingbird

up

up

these pieces
make a puzzle
full of
colors
shapes
and words

do you see . . .

frog by pig by circle?
chicken over square?
guppy under hummingbird
and yellow next to bear?

circle under berry

berry over square

circle over berry
under orange
over square